# colours of australia

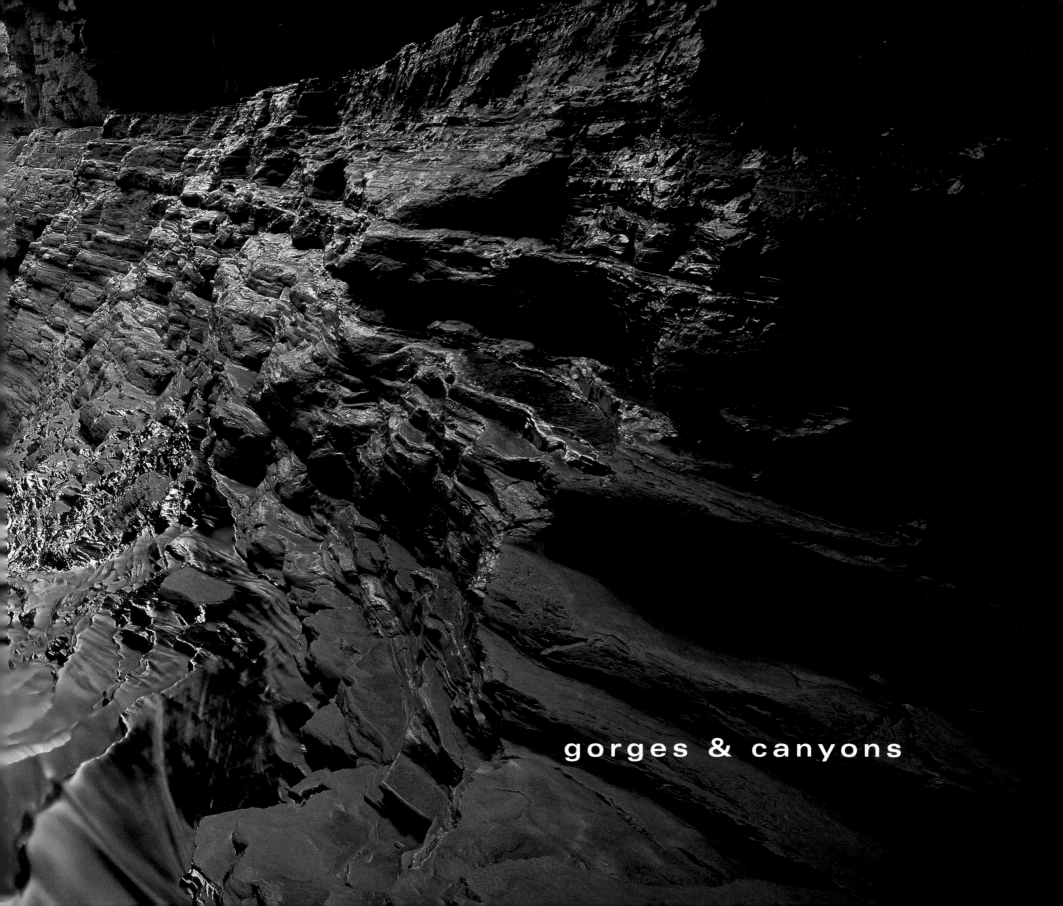

gorges & canyons

# gorges & canyons

The Taoists of ancient China regarded water as a metaphor for the ideal life. Water always yields, the sages observed, yet rocks and mountains inevitably succumb to its patient power. It speaks for water's humble strength that its influence can be seen right across this dry continent in gorges, ravines and canyons worn through solid rock by what often looks like an impossibly small stream, or by brief flushes of floodwater over an immense sprawl of aeons.

Climbing to summits for the view is a favourite occupation in younger lands. On this old continent, with its worn stubs of mountain ranges, some of the best scenery requires a descent. The red-and-gold rock and spinifex landscape of the Pilbara – for instance – has a memorable majesty, but the most enduring memories of many visitors to this remote region are painted in rich dark ochres and oxide blues: the colours of the magnificent gorges that gash the Hamersley Range. These are natural cathedrals, impressive for their scale and architecture. The impression of something sacred quivers in the receptive hush that seems suspended between rock walls.

For Aboriginal people, this sacredness was deeper than fancy. Any list of the continent's gorges – Katherine, Lawn Hill, Mossman, Geikie, Kings Canyon – describes sources of life. The seasonal journeys of the tribespeople orbited around these great natural cisterns. Because of the water they almost invariably hold, the gorges are natural larders, too. At Carnarvon Gorge in central Queensland, 173 bird species have been recorded. It's known that Aboriginal people were visiting this natural cathedral for at least 17,000 years before Christ was born. Today, gorges like Carnarvon are again sites of pilgrimage. But instead of life in the form of food and water, visitors take away images and impressions to renew their spirit.

Not all pilgrimages are equal in rigour. Thousands take the easy drive to Katherine Gorge, in the Northern Territory, and from cruise boats photograph the towering walls. Few are now deterred from visiting more out-of-the-way gorges at the end of dirt roads, like the fossil-studded clefts in the Flinders Ranges of South Australia or the waterfall-laced chasm of Bell Gorge in the Kimberley. But there remain places less well discovered. The eastern fall of the Great Dividing Range is sliced along its length with magnificent gorges, some of them only available to the pilgrim with a pack and sturdy boots. There are gorges most places there are ranges and rock and water. Getting to them often means getting away from everything else. Once there, though, nothing is required of the visitor but, as the Taoists suggest, simply being.

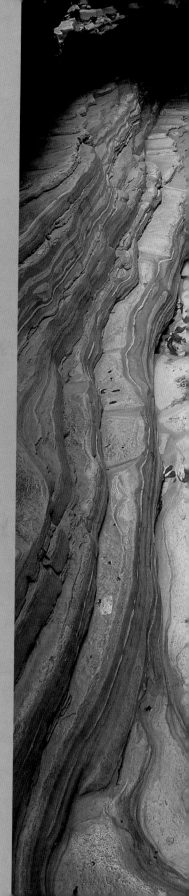

*pages 14–15*

**HANCOCK GORGE, KARIJINI NP, WA**

The hiss of icy waters echoes through Hancock Gorge as they cascade towards a sunlit pool. When the sun strikes the gorge's upper walls, the water acts like a giant reflector, setting the entire chamber below alight. Negotiating Karijini's narrow gorges makes you feel that you're journeying to the centre of the Earth: passages seem to lead forever downwards through rock rich in iron and asbestos.

*page 16*

**GEIKIE GORGE NP, WA**

As the sun dips over the nearby Oscar Range, the wind drops and the Fitzroy River turns glassy, mirroring the burnt hues of Geikie Gorge. The river has created this 7 km long gorge by cutting through the soft limestone of an ancient barrier reef. In the wet season it can become a wild torrent, rising at least 15 m above its dry-season level and leaving a distinctive white band on the rock.

*right*

**COLO GORGE, WOLLEMI NP, NSW**

Deep in one of Australia's wildest and least accessible regions, the Colo River cuts through a landscape that encapsulates the spirit of Wollemi National Park. The park conserves a bush-covered sandstone massif criss-crossed with gorges, canyons and valleys – and very few roads – only two hours from Sydney, Australia's biggest city. Thirty kilometres long and up to 300 m deep, the Colo Gorge is best explored by canoe.

*left*

**YARDIE CREEK GORGE, CAPE RANGE NP, WA**

The pink flush of dawn and the faint hues of a distant rainbow complement the iron-rich reds of Yardie Creek Gorge. At this early hour you can hear the gorge echoing with the falsetto calls of the little corellas that nest in hollows in the rock. This place is also a haven for the black-footed rock wallaby, once common but now confined to isolated pockets.

*right*

**KINGS CANYON, WATARRKA NP, NT**

In the heat of the afternoon sun the surface of Kings Canyon's walls reflect the outback colours of central Australia. Rough-hewn and inhospitable though it looks, this spectacular canyon and other gullies in the surrounding landscape shelter a rich collection of plants. On the canyon floor the aptly named Garden of Eden is a welcome oasis of lush vegetation and cool, clear rock pools.

*page 22 top*

**WINDJANA GORGE, WINDJANA GORGE NP, WA**

Dwarfed by the rugged scenery it has created, the Lennard River curves past the towering limestone walls of Windjana Gorge. The river has carved this 4 km long canyon through a fossilised coral reef and on hot Kimberley days the walls provide a cool refuge for plants, corellas and fruit bats. You're likely to see freshwater crocodiles basking on the beaches.

*page 22 bottom*

**ORMISTON GORGE, WEST MACDONNELL NP, NT**

An ancient tree survives beside a waterhole at the mouth of Ormiston Gorge, one of the most magnificent gorges in central Australia. In summer, when the temperature climbs into the 40s, visitors head for the park's many permanent waterholes, where the water is deep and very cold. A world-class walking track, the Larapinta Trail, runs through much of the park.

*page 23 top*

**THE GORGE, MOUNT BUFFALO NP, VIC**

While valleys far below still lie in gloom, the walls of The Gorge, one of Mount Buffalo's most visited features, light up in the first rays of sunrise. Towering 1000 m above the surrounding lowlands, the mountain is an island in the sky that often floats on a sea of cloud. Its plateau is dotted with crags and tors set amid woodlands and snowgrass meadows.

*page 23 bottom*

**INDARRI WATERFALL, LAWN HILL (BOODJAMULLA) NP, QLD**

The emerald-green waters of Lawn Hill Creek tumble from the upper section of Lawn Hill Gorge into Middle Gorge at Indarri Waterfall. At its base the waterfall forms a natural spa pool where you can have an invigorating swim on even the hottest days. The creek sustains lush waterside stands of Livistona palms and pandanus but less than 100 m from the gorge, the vegetation quickly thins and withers.

*left*

**DUWADARRI WATERHOLE, LAWN HILL NP, QLD**

Not a ripple stirs the dark surface of Duwadarri Waterhole, in the middle section of Lawn Hill Gorge, before the morning breeze springs up. Here, as in its other sections, Lawn Hill Creek is rich in freshwater animal life, including two turtle species and more than 20 types of fish. This abundant aquatic life provides a feast for the resident freshwater crocodiles, like the magnificent specimen below.

*above*

**GEIKIE GORGE NP, WA**

Bearing scars that show the enormous height of wet-season floods, the limestone walls of Geikie Gorge are scoured to a chalk-white. Although the gorge is more than 300 km from the coast you might see rays and sawfish here. These saltwater fish long ago adapted to fresh water and share this stretch of the Fitzroy River with more typical Kimberley river dwellers such as barramundi and freshwater crocodiles.

*right*

**SPA POOL, KARIJINI NP, WA**

Flowing into a seemingly bottomless pool of the deepest sapphire, a small creek in Karijini National Park has carved a shape of perfect symmetry in the rock. The water in the aptly named Spa Pool is icy cold and, after a long hike, it's hard to resist diving in. The blue colour of the gorge is caused by traces of blue asbestos in the rock.

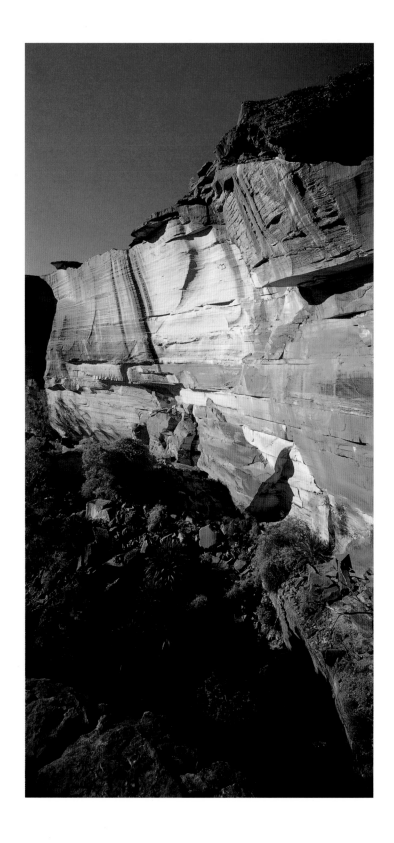

*page 34 left*

**HANCOCK GORGE, KARIJINI NP, WA**

When the temperature in the open is up in the high 30s, cool passages like this one well below ground level are a delight to explore. Direct sunlight penetrates to the gorge floor for only a brief time each day.

*page 34 right*

**FORTESCUE FALLS, KARIJINI NP, WA**

Enticing spring-fed waters tumble over Fortescue Falls, at Dales Gorge, into a pool that's home to fish and turtles. This is a refreshing place for a swim on a hot Pilbara day.

*page 35 left*

**KINGS CANYON, WATARRKA NP, NT**

A geological masterpiece that's unique in the NT, Kings Canyon burns impossibly red in the last rays of day. Water entering fractures in the sandstone, which show as black marks, eventually causes blocks of the rock to fall from the wall.

*page 35 right*

**HANCOCK GORGE, KARIJINI NP, WA**

A pool 100 m below ground level catches the last light as it's reflected downwards from the top of Hancock Gorge. For a photographer, waiting for this moment means climbing out in the dark.

*right*

**GRAND CANYON, BLUE MOUNTAINS NP, NSW**

Ferns, mosses and aerial roots festoon the perpetually dripping walls of the 100 m deep Grand Canyon in the Blue Mountains. Occasionally overhangs break away and fall in an explosion of bark and leaves. In pools like the one in the foreground you're likely to see bright orange yabbies up to 15 cm long.

_left_

**CARNARVON GORGE, CARNARVON NP, QLD**

Even the tallest palms look like miniatures beneath Parrabooya, one of the most majestic walls in the Carnarvon Gorge system. It takes a 10 km walk to reach this point but the view of the near-white precipice sandstone peculiar to this area is stunning. The 30 km long gorge is densely forested. Carnarvon Creek supports a large platypus population and if you walk quietly near the water you may be lucky enough to spot one or two.

_right_

**HAMERSLEY GORGE, KARIJINI NP, WA**

An intense cobalt blue sky provides a stunning contrast to the rust-red cliff tops of Hamersley Gorge on the western side of Karijini National Park. Seemingly impossible forces have bent this rock wall into a contortion of buckled waves that display the iron-rich rock's bands of reds, oranges, mustard yellows and dusky whites. Striking snappy gums have taken root in the weathered cliff; the stream has polished the substratum to a smooth blue-grey.

**NITMILUK NP, NT**

Fast flowing rapids and rock bars link the third and second gorges in Nitmiluk, or Katherine, Gorge. All the gorges are separated by rapids but it's possible to canoe up to the ninth gorge. Along the way you'll find campsites on sandy beaches. In some places the river is 30 m deep and is surrounded by tall cliffs with angular walls, sheer cracks and crevasses.

### BELL GORGE, KIMBERLEY, WA

A liquid stairway leads to the burnished dome at the top of beautiful Bell Gorge. Situated near the mid-section of the Gibb River Road, Bell Gorge provides a cool and relaxing place to swim and enjoy the classic scenery of the rugged Kimberley. During wet-season storms the waters rush over the falls but in the dry months the flow is reduced to a gentle trickle.

*left*

**HANCOCK GORGE, KARIJINI NP, WA**

A shining tiger's eye stares out of a shallow pool on the floor of Hancock Gorge. The illusion can be seen for only a short time each day when a rock face at the top of the gorge is lit by the setting sun. The high-sided gorge is narrow, in places only a metre wide, and to reach this point it's necessary to walk with one foot on each slippery side. The beautiful blue stripes in the gorge are caused by blue asbestos in the iron-rich walls.

*right*

**VIOLET GORGE, CARNARVON NP, QLD**

Water percolating through porous sandstone has created a fairytale scene of green in the midst of a harsh land. At the Moss Garden, in Violet Gorge, water drips from the walls onto moss, ferns, liverworts and hornworts that cling to the overhangs and floor. The air is alive with the croaking of frogs and the eye always catches movement here, as dainty fronds dip and rebound with the impact of drops.

*right*

**KOOLPIN GORGE (JARRANGBARNMI),
KAKADU NP, NT**

In a series of dark pools, Koolpin Creek drops step by step
from the Arnhem Land Plateau to Kakadu's lowlands. Some
of the pools are 50–80 m across and very deep. During the
Wet they link up in a single thundering maelstrom and, over
the aeons, Koolpin Gorge has been carved deep into the
plateau for many kilometres. The gorge is a limited-access,
permit-only area. At times you might have it all to yourself.

*below*

**KOOLPIN CREEK, KAKADU NP, NT**

Mysterious figures speak from the deep past in the hundreds
of rock art sites that dot Kakadu. This one is on the walls of an
overhang in the gorge carved by Koolpin Creek, on the edge of
the Arnhem Land Plateau.

rivers & lakes

# rivers & lakes

The branching paths of rivers and streams and the swellings of lakes etch the
Australian map like a diagram of the land's arteries. The reality can be both less and
more than the maps indicate. Many of the country's waterways cycle between brief
plenty and extended nothing. Major rivers may be dry dusty channels. A small gully
may overflow with floodwaters a kilometre wide. And it can all change in hours.

The first British colonisers, used to the unceasing flow of European waters, had
trouble with the notion of a river that sometimes wasn't. Botanist Joseph Banks
in 1798 expressed a typically naive view: "It is impossible to conceive that such a
large body of land, as large as all Europe, does not produce vast rivers, capable of
being navigated into the heart of the interior…". After decades of exploration, the
colonisers came to accept the impossible. Australians instead learned to celebrate
the miracle of billabongs, lively with fish and raucous with white cockatoos.

It is a different story for the waterways of the north and east fringes. Here some
waters always run. When a monsoon dumps into the red Kimberley ranges drained
by the Fitzroy River, the torrent that rages down the craggy river gorges would
be capable of filling Sydney Harbour in a few tumultuous hours. Springs feed the
everlasting jade ribbon of the reedy Gregory River as it winds through a savannah
landscape, en route to losing itself in the Gulf of Carpentaria. In summer, the Snowy
Mountains' cap of winter snow chatters off the mountain flanks down steep rocky
streams, finding its various ways into the Murray River to sustain stately groves of
red river gums. And in Tasmania, peat-brown waters lie between walls of dark scrub,
seemingly immobile in wider stretches, but forced into sudsy rapids in the narrows.

However remote these fruitful places seem to be from the dry gullies and blinding
saltpans of the deep inland, there is an unseen connection. When intermittent
floods feel their way down the inland waterways to spread out across lakes
and marshes, something is invisibly communicated. The signal is understood by
pelicans, black swans, snipe, spoonbills – even waders from Siberia – living on more
reliable waterways on the continent's fringe. Within days they have found their
way thousands of kilometres to Lake Eyre or the Macquarie Marshes or another
temporary oasis of the outback, and have flung themselves into an avian orgy. The
birds stuff themselves on the flood-borne explosion of fish and crustaceans, and
mate. And when the lakes disappear, new generations of birds depart to grace
coastal inlets, always ready for the call out of the wide dry inland.

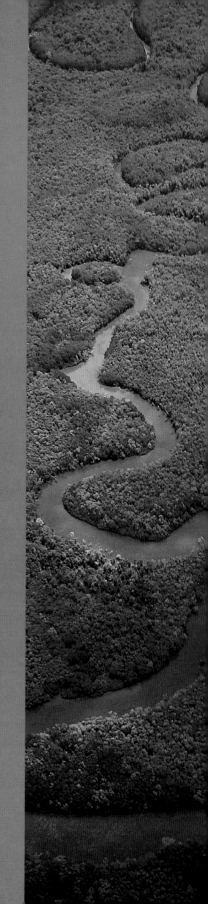

*pages 46–47*

**SNOWY RIVER, NSW**

Polished boulders on the banks of the Snowy River near the
NSW–Victoria border show how high the water used to rise
when its thundering rapids were awe-inspiring. Today it's
quieter but still fast-flowing, tumbling over rapids that are
a challenge for canoeists. Before it was dammed in 1962
the Snowy carried more water than any other river in NSW.

*page 48*

**WALLIS LAKE, NSW**

Clouds build in a brooding sky over an old wooden skiff that
has been abandoned after many a useful year. The old craft
rests in the gentle shallows of Wallis Lake, south of Forster.
The lake has the largest single area of seagrass in the state
and you can see many migratory birds here, including the
endangered little tern.

*right*

**PENTECOST RIVER, WA**

Inlaid like gunmetal into the Kimberley landscape, a deep
waterhole on the Pentecost River lies motionless on a warm,
dry-season afternoon. During the Wet, downpours can cause
the river to swell and quickly cover the banks. At waterholes
like this one on El Questro Station, barramundi are plentiful.
So are saltwater crocodiles, even though this part of the river
is many kilometres from the river's mouth near Wyndham.

**DUNNS SWAMP, WOLLEMI NP, NSW**

The screech of purple swamp hens and the calls of myriad
other water birds punctuate the dawn as the rising sun burns
the mist from Dunns Swamp. Set among bush-clad hills and
rock formations known as pagodas on the western edge
of Wollemi, this lake was created by the damming of the
Cudgegong River in 1930. Paddling a canoe on these waters
with their stunning surroundings is a memorable experience.

### TWIN FALLS, KAKADU NP, NT

Wispy ribbons of silver cascade down the rugged face of Twin Falls in a remote part of Kakadu National Park. You can reach this point, your first view of the falls, by swimming and wading along a creek. A long trip by 4WD, on a track that includes a deep-water crossing, is the start of your journey. The warm waters of the pandanus-lined creek are full of fish.

*left*

**DAINTREE NP, QLD**

A rivulet gurgles through the rainforest of Mossman Gorge, in the southernmost of Daintree National Park's two sections. The vegetation here is so dense that often the only way to penetrate it is to follow small streams like this one. The park is a vital component of the Wet Tropics World Heritage Area, which contains the highest concentration of families of ancient flowering plants in the world.

*right*

**RAPID RIVER, TARKINE WILDERNESS, TAS**

Myrtles and ferns crowd near the dark waters of Rapid River, in the Tarkine Wilderness. Floods have scoured and smoothed fallen trees and left their distorted shapes in heaps. The banks are dotted with small mud chimneys, which tiny freshwater burrowing crayfish create at the entrances to their burrows. The world's largest freshwater invertebrate, the Tasmanian giant crayfish, lives here too.

*following pages*

**WILLIAMS RIVER, BARRINGTON TOPS NP, NSW**

A shallow stretch of the Williams River runs over smooth river stones. Here, in its lower reaches, the river flows between densely forested banks but higher in its course it drops and tumbles steeply, flowing through a landscape of subalpine grassland and stands of snow gums.

*page 60 left*

**HAWKESBURY RIVER, KU-RING-GAI CHASE NP, NSW**

Driftwood lies on the yellow sandstone platforms that line the banks of the Hawkesbury River estuary. Steep woodland ridges plunge into the brackish waters where the river is edged with grass trees and pink angophoras. Most of the park is thick woodland; travelling by boat gives the best view of the river.

*page 60 right*

**SURPRISE RIVER, FRANKLIN–GORDON WILD RIVERS NP, TAS**

Swollen by rain, the waters of the Surprise River race through the cool Tasmanian rainforest to their meeting with the Franklin River. They then tumble into a series of narrow canyons and gorges on their way to the Gordon River and, eventually, Macquarie Harbour.

*page 61 left*

**PIEMAN RIVER, ARTHUR–PIEMAN CA, TAS**

A magnificent huon pine stoops low to the Pieman River, which marks the southern boundary of the Arthur–Pieman Conservation Area. Huon pines, which can live for thousands of years, are often found reaching out like this over water.

*page 61 right*

**WANGGOOLBA CREEK, FRASER ISLAND, QLD**

Perfectly clear and totally pure, the water of Wanggoolba Creek flows like liquid glass over its bed of immaculate sand. Edged by palms, the creek flows to the western coast of Fraser Island, the world's biggest sand island.

*left*

**LAKE JINDABYNE, NSW**

On a crisp alpine morning, Lake Jindabyne lies like a piece of fallen sky outside the eastern edge of Kosciuszko National Park. Created in the 1960s by the damming of the Snowy River, the lake is 930 m above sea level and its cold waters provide a good habitat for trout.

*left*

**WARREN RIVER, WARREN NP, WA**

The sun breaks over the horizon and lights the mist-filled valley with a smoky orange glow. As day begins, this Warren River valley echoes with the raucous laugh of kookaburras and the twittering of fairy wrens. The river, near the town of Pemberton, flows through deep valleys filled with magnificent old-growth karri trees.

*right*

**LAKE DOVE, CRADLE MOUNTAIN–LAKE ST CLAIR NP, TAS**

A crisp, silent and breathless morning polishes the surface of Lake Dove, creating a perfect mirror for the castle-like crags of Cradle Mountain. When the water is this calm it's easy to spot the bow wave of a platypus as it searches for yabbies. Lake Dove is at the northern end of the Overland Track.

*left*

**FLORENCE FALLS, LITCHFIELD NP, NT**

In the glow of evening, reflected sunlight casts a golden sheen across the plunge pool at the base of Florence Falls in Litchfield National Park. Numerous spring-fed creeks tumble from the Tabletop Range and rainforest fills the valleys and gullies that are watered by them. They provide a haven for a variety of creatures, such as little red flying foxes (below).

*right*

**CEPHISSUS CREEK, CRADLE MOUNTAIN–LAKE ST CLAIR NP, TAS**

Filling Pine Valley with the roar of its rushing waters, Cephissus Creek pours over a series of rock shelves on its way to join the Narcissus River, which eventually flows into Lake St Clair. The creek drains the uplands of the Du Cane Range, which lies to the west of the Overland Track. King Billy pines, myrtles and pandani *(Richea pandanifolia)* flourish in the moist conditions.

_pages 70–71_

**WATER MISCELLANY**

Whatever form it takes, water on a dry continent has a particularly mesmeric magic. These four waterways are no exception. Page 70 top: a bend in the Murray River Reserve near Cobram, Victoria, mirrors the red gums lining the bank. Page 70 bottom: the slow-flowing waters of the Fortescue River reflect the pink blush of sunset in Millstream–Chichester National Park, WA. Page 71 top: broad Sandy Billabong in Kakadu National Park, NT, is a gathering place for birds during the Dry. Page 71 bottom: the Darling River, one of Australia's great outback waterways, flows beside Kinchega National Park, NSW.

_left_

**WOLLONDILLY RIVER, NSW**

Skirting the southern edge of the Blue Mountains National Park, the Wollondilly River meanders peacefully between river oaks and eucalypts. It's an ideal habitat for the platypus, yabbies and eels that thrive here. Wombats (below) live here too and you're likely to see many large burrows along the river's banks.

beaches, bays & islands

# beaches, bays & islands

East, west, north and south, Australia falls away into seas with temperaments as different as the colours of their waters. Land and ocean meet along more than 30,000 kilometres and across latitudes that range from equatorial to the Roaring Forties. Seen piecemeal, with its mangroves and seabirds, cliffs and sands, spray-spattered lighthouses and tropical islands, Australia's coastline could be the shores of many countries, not just that of one sprawling island-continent.

To the east and west, long azure swells roll in from the expanses of the world's two biggest oceans, beating out the maritime pulse of three States. In the north, mangrove swamps and tidal flats lie along the margins of the emerald-green Timor and Arafura seas – benign waters, except when thrashed by monsoonal cyclones. And to the south lie the chilly, temperamental waters of the Southern Ocean: clear and glittering with a sapphire blue under sunlight; grey, grim and vengeful in a winter storm.

Australians are a littoral people. They live, labour and play largely on the continent's fringes, between these multi-hued oceans and the red outback. Just as relatively few Australians travel into the sprawling inland, few sail beyond the shore. They prefer to cluster along the shoreline, easing the pressure of life with the continual presence of water. And why not, in a country so prodigally endowed with coastal habitats?

These shores present faces that include the inhospitable, but the inhospitable can be inviting – like Victoria's west coast, where cliffs and bays are coursed by the spectacular Great Ocean Road. For the motorist leisurely stopping by the island pillars of the Twelve Apostles, the sight of a slavering sea leaping up wave-gnawed rock is a photogenic spectacle. It presented an entirely different sight to those in sailing ships driven by the Roaring Forties into the mouth of Bass Strait. "I have seldom seen a more fearful section of coastline" wrote 18th century navigator Matthew Flinders. Nor, presumably, had those on the 160-odd ships lost along this beautiful, wild shore.

Australia's feared coasts have been largely tamed. Cape Byron, mainland Australia's most easterly point, had claimed at least 16 ships before a lighthouse was installed there in 1903. Today, the lighthouse stands over a coastline celebrated for beauty rather than danger and a community largely dedicated to getting back in touch with nature. But it doesn't matter which part of the coast it is. At the coast, everyday Australia stops – and everything else becomes possible. The coast is the nation's transforming edge; an ever-present reminder that Australia is an island.

*pages 74–75*

**THE LAGOON, NINGALOO MARINE PARK, WA**

With a tongue of foam, the Indian Ocean licks the soft white sands of The Lagoon, a shallow bay opposite the southern end of Ningaloo Reef. In summer female green turtles come ashore here to lay their eggs and, in the dark waters beyond the reef, whale sharks cruise regularly in search of food.

*page 76*

**HAT HEAD NP, NSW**

Like a giant shark fin, Korogoro Point juts into the sea from Hat Head, on the mid-north coast of NSW. It's a strenuous climb to the headland's summit but, at 164 m above sea level, you then have a stunning 360-degree view and it's perfect for whale watching. You can hear the roar from the caves below the headland as they're pounded by the swell.

*right*

**ELIM BEACH, CAPE YORK PENINSULA, QLD**

A glowing palette of warm hues surrounds a dune of white silica sand shimmering above the tropical green of the Coral Sea. The sand is so fine and pure that it squeaks underfoot. On the horizon at left of centre is the flat-topped headland of Cape Bedford.

**FITZROY ISLAND, GREAT BARRIER REEF, QLD**

The start of a perfect day in paradise. High tide covers the
sands of Nudey Beach, Fitzroy Island, in the Coral Sea 35 km
east of Cairns. Coral bommies teeming with marine life can be
seen as dark patches just off the beach. In the early morning
giant trevally sometimes round up huge schools of small fish,
driving them relentlessly into the shore.

**TWO PEOPLES BAY, WA**

A sensational day highlights the timeless perfection of a dynamic southern ocean seascape. Two Peoples Bay, east of Albany, epitomises the classic colours of the southern Australian seascapes – green rolling hills peppered with orange granite outcrops and pure-white squeaky sand that enhances the dazzling blue of the clean ocean waters.

*following pages*

**WINEGLASS BAY, FREYCINET NP, TAS**

The dazzling sickle of sand in Wineglass Bay, on Freycinet Peninsula's east coast, has become a pilgrimage destination for many visitors to Tasmania. It's a magical place with its long sweep of sand and crystal-clear water. The three-hour walk to the summit of Mount Amos, where this picture was taken, is steep and involves a great deal of rock-scrambling.

*above*

**THISTLE COVE, CAPE LE GRAND NP, WA**

Like the end of the world approaching, a cloud of smoke and ash from a bushfire looms over Thistle Cove, in Cape Le Grand National Park, near Esperance, WA. Usually a dazzling blue, the water took on an unusual aquamarine hue when the sky was filled with this intense black and purple cloud.

*right*

**THE BASIN, ROTTNEST ISLAND, WA**

A fiery dawn, heralding an approaching storm, sets sky and sea ablaze at The Basin, Rottnest Island. This is one of the many swimming and snorkelling spots that rim the island, which lies 19 km off Fremantle. Beneath the waters there are caves and swim-throughs that are quite spectacular.

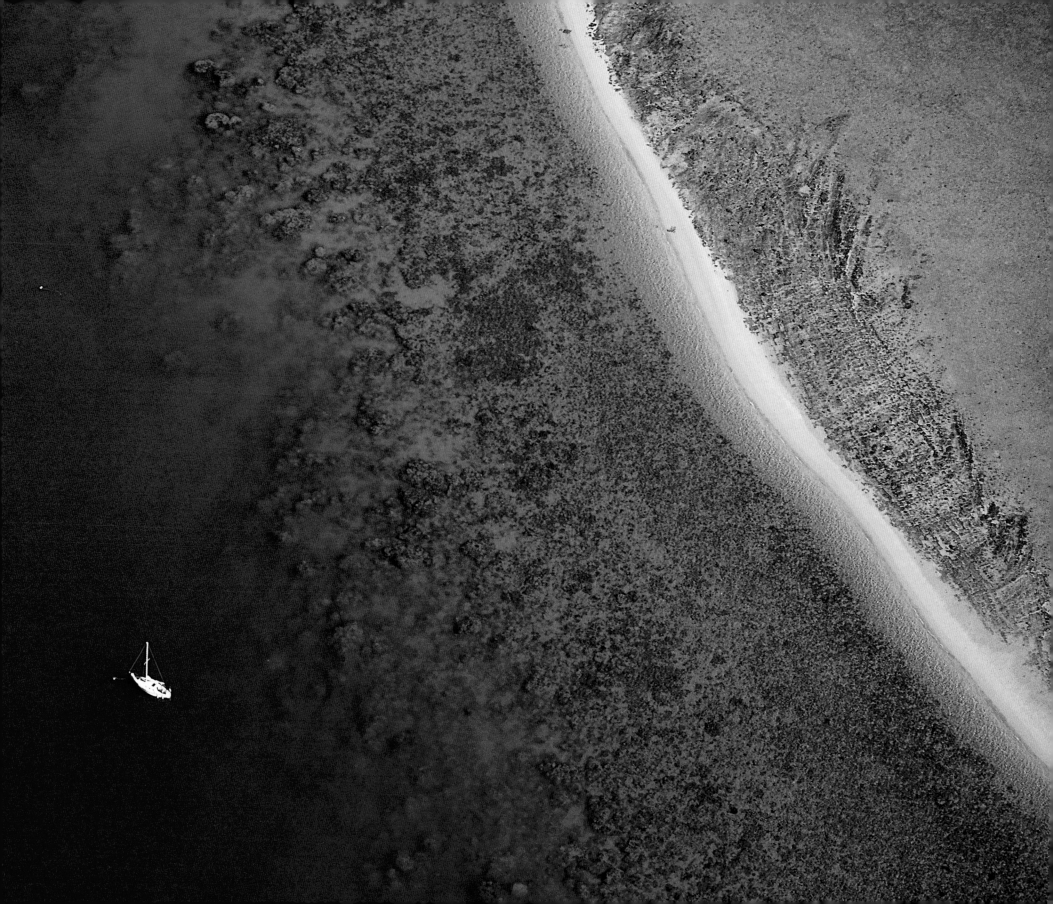

*left*

**WHITSUNDAY ISLAND, GREAT BARRIER REEF, QLD**

Hues merge in swirls of colour as the tide ebbs sinuously from Hill Inlet, on Whitsunday Island, between banks of fine white silica sand. The island is part of the east coast's largest island chain. The magnificent 7 km sweep of Whitehaven Beach leads the eye to the islands of the Lindeman Group in the distance.

*right*

**GREAT SANDY NP, FRASER ISLAND, QLD**

Sea blends into sky in a brilliant display of red, yellow and orange, with Indian Head, the easternmost point on Fraser Island, shown in silhouette. Captain Cook named the rocky headland after spotting a gathering of Aboriginals here in 1770. From the top of the headland you can often see large sharks cruising not far offshore.

*left*

**PEBBLY BEACH, MURRAMARANG NP, NSW**

As if checking out the surf, an eastern grey kangaroo hops onto Pebbly Beach in the mid-section of Murramarang National Park, on the south coast of nsw. Mobs of kangaroos are drawn to these beaches by the sweet, dew-rich grass that has been planted to bind the dunes. At times they venture further out onto the sand to nibble seaweed. The park is a beachcomber's delight, its rock shelves full of sea-urchins, crabs and shells.

*right*

**AUSTRALIA'S SEASHORES**

Shores can make grand scenes, but the variety and beauty of their detail transports the viewer into unimagined dimensions. Clockwise from top left: seaweed at Mount William National Park, Tasmania; a dead leaf and coral fragments washed up on Fitzroy Island, Qld; a clam shell on Ningaloo Reef, wa; a feather and krill at Torndirrup National Park, near Albany, wa.

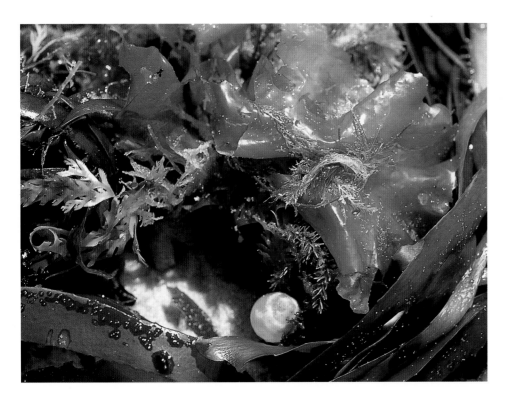

*right*

**CROAJINGOLONG NP, VIC**

A celestial warning signal, this bright orange flash from a rainbow off the coast of Croajingolong was the prelude to a vicious storm that tore apart the fleet of yachts taking part in the Sydney to Hobart race in 1998. On the south-eastern cusp of the Australian continent, Croajingolong lies where Bass Strait meets the Tasman Sea. The weather here can be fickle, and there's many a shipwreck to prove it.

*page 102 left*

**NINGALOO MARINE PARK, WA**

A dazzling dune spills into the inviting waters of Ningaloo Marine Park south of Coral Bay. Here Ningaloo Reef is close to the shore, and at low tide you can walk out to its seaward edge. If you're lucky you may see humpback whales just beyond the breakers.

*page 102 right*

**CHILI BEACH, IRON RANGE NP, QLD**

Coconuts litter the foreshore of Chili Beach, in Iron Range National Park, about 240 km south of Cape York. Drinking the juice of a freshly picked nut is a delight, but swimming here is unwise as sharks regularly patrol the shallows.

*page 103 left*

**ARAGUNNU BEACH, MIMOSA ROCKS NP, NSW**

A muted dawn breaks on Aragunnu Beach in the northern section of Mimosa Rocks National Park, 23 km south of Bermagui. As each wave breaks, the bay echoes with the rattle of myriad pebbles being tossed against one another.

*page 103 right*

**RUSSELL ISLAND, GREAT BARRIER REEF, QLD**

Relic from the ocean depths, a spiralled nautilus shell lies beached on the shore of Russell Island. Related to squids and cuttlefish, the nautilus lives in deep tropical water off the edges of reefs but rises to shallower water at night to feed.

*left*

**CAPE HAUY, TASMAN NP, TAS**

On a melancholy morning, the bastions of Cape Hauy, on the eastern shore of the Tasman Peninsula, rise like the ruins of an ancient castle from the Tasman Sea. The island in the distance, Hippolyte Rocks, lies 4 km away. This view is only possible if you're prepared to get perilously close to the edge of the cliff.

*right*

**SLEEPY BAY, FREYCINET NP, TAS**

Dabs of brilliant orange and green, created by lichen and moss growing on the tumble of granite boulders, brighten the otherwise sombre shoreline of Sleepy Bay. On a moody morning like this, the small inlet stirs all the senses – with the tang of the sea, the scuttling of crabs, the yelping of gulls and the feel of velvety rain on the skin. Shrouded in damp mist in the distance is Mount Parsons.

*left*

### CAPE LEVEQUE, KIMBERLEY COAST, WA

As though glowing with the heat they've absorbed all day, these fantastically weathered cliffs stand at Cape Leveque, or Kooljaman, on the northern tip of Dampier Land peninsula. Storms, wind-blown sand and 8 m tides have helped erode the cliffs into these shapes. Their deep, warm colour contrasts with the cream-coloured sand and the milky turquoise water.

*page 108 top*

### BYRON BAY, NSW

Surfers enjoy small waves in the clear waters off Wategos Beach. The north-facing beach at the edge of Byron Bay has consistently good waves, which surfers frequently share with pods of dolphins that cruise the coast. The headland here is a great location for whale watching.

*page 108 bottom*

### CANAL ROCKS, LEEUWIN–NATURALISTE NP, WA

A heavy ocean swell smashes into the outer wall of Canal Rocks and creates a maelstrom of swirling waters in the narrow canal. The rocks, near Yallingup, are exposed to the full force of the sea. This part of the coast is notorious for the large swells that roll in from the open ocean to the west.

*page 109 top*

### WILSONS PROMONTORY, VIC

High tide at Sealers Cove leaves only a thin strip of sand on the huge bay surrounded by peaks. At low tide the beach is a broad band of sand. This cove, where you can step from the beach straight into the forest, is the first stop on a three-day 36 km hike that is one of the most stunning coastal walks in Australia.

*page 109 bottom*

### COFFIN BAY NP, SA

White rollers wash across the blue waters of Avoid Bay on the western side of Coffin Bay. The chilly southern waters can be rough at times and crayfishing boats sometimes anchor in the bay during bad weather. Dolphins splash in this bay and many bird species frequent the beaches.

*left*

**FRANÇOIS PERON NP, SHARK BAY, WA**

A dune near the northern tip of Peron Peninsula, in the centre of Shark Bay, dips a white-hot finger into the sea. Bottlenose dolphins have made this area famous. Further south is Monkey Mia, a small settlement with a campsite, where the dolphins have been coming close to the shore to mingle with people since at least 1964.

*above*

**LADY MUSGRAVE ISLAND, GREAT BARRIER REEF, QLD**

Adrift on a mosaic of blues, Lady Musgrave Island is surrounded by more than 1200 ha of living coral and has one of the most beautiful deepwater lagoons of all the Great Barrier Reef's islands. One of the reef's southernmost coral cays, it's covered in pisonia forest where black noddies nest.

## CAPE ARNHEM (NANYDJAKA), ARNHEM LAND, NT

Projecting between scalloped beaches, one of two headlands known as the twin eagles, or Gaynada, catches the afternoon light on Cape Arnhem, Arnhem Land's easternmost point. The sea around the cape is clear and blue, with occasional coral outcrops, and is home to saltwater crocodiles (below). Salties, the world's largest crocodiles, are fearsome predators, able to move with extraordinary speed.

forests

# forests

"I love a sunburnt country / A land of sweeping plains", Dorothea Mackellar wrote in her paean to Australia, "My Country". These words and the stanza's closing line, "The wide brown land for me!" have become a popular potted summary of Australia. Like many photographic representations of the country, this depiction neglects the forests. Australia's forests are, like so much of this country, unique. They are magnificent without being grandiose, mysterious without lurking terrors.

Mackellar didn't ignore the trees. Her next stanza begins: "The stark white ring-barked forests / All tragic to the moon...". White Australians were in the middle of their conquest of the bush when Mackellar wrote her poem in 1904. It took another 80-odd years for the nation to realise that the victory might be too thorough. The forests that do remain are often those that cover slopes deemed too inaccessible to log or clear. Others have been only recently locked away from the saws. And many have been logged, sometimes for generations, but stand nevertheless.

What is left of Australia's original forests is wonderful in its variety. In the south stand forests of soaring splendour. Tasmania grows the swamp gum or mountain ash, the tallest flowering plant in the world when, after three centuries or so, it reaches heights of more than 95 metres. In south-west Western Australia, the karri bolts to heights of up to 90 metres in a mere century. To be in either place, puny against these mighty living columns, is to see nature's power made manifest. Along the southern half of the Great Dividing Range lie the dry and wet sclerophyll forests that could be seen as typical of Australian timberlands – if there was anything typical about the forests themselves. Statuesque eucalypts, tree ferns and light filtered through the smoky blues of gum oils are characteristics of forests like those of the Yarra Ranges, the Otway Ranges, and the World Heritage-listed flanks of New England. But each Great Divide forest contains other places: gullies thick with rainforest; dry western slopes where trees are scattered through grasslands; meadows in clearings; thick heaths beside mossy waterways.

And there are the wet forests of the far north, like the celebrated Daintree. In the south, the big trees appear engaged in an orderly competition for light; in the tropical rainforest, it is a tangled struggle, fig against liana, palm on fern. These northern botanical arks are a window on prehistory, a glimpse of this land before the conquering march of the eucalypt. But all history is irrelevant to the forests themselves; it is their future that counts.

*pages 114–115*

**NEW ENGLAND NP, NSW**

Mist rolls in from the edge of an abyss, rendering the normally brightly coloured trunks of snow gums in a monochromatic mauve blush. The gums grow densely on the edge of the plateau near this World Heritage-listed park's highest point. This mist gathered in the evening when the temperature plummeted and the forest was filled with an eerie silence.

*page 116*

**BORDER RANGES NP, NSW**

The brilliant greens surrounding Brindle Creek, in the upper reaches of the Border Ranges National Park, shine like a multi-faceted emerald. The rugged area's high rainfall fosters dense growth. Light rain enhances the greens of the vegetation, such as the metre-long leaves of the *Helmholtzia* lilies, the epiphytes in the trees and the moss that covers almost every rock.

*right*

**ALPINE NP, VIC**

The colourful trunks of mountain ash crowd the steep slopes of Mount Stirling, in Victoria's alpine area. In winter the trees are often dusted with snow. The thick forests are home to feathertail and sugar gliders, mountain brushtail and ringtail possums. The calls of gang-gang cockatoos echo across the valleys by day, and powerful owls hunt here at night.

*page 120 left*

**FRANKLIN–GORDON WILD RIVERS NP, TAS**

Like camouflaged faces peering from the forest, moss-clad burls decorate a veteran myrtle near the Franklin River. The tree typifies the Tasmanian rainforests, where every space is covered with thick moss and vines.

*page 120 right*

**FREYCINET NP, TAS**

The trunk of a eucalypt mirrors the colours of the pink granite against which it grows. Eucalypt forests grow between the shore and the park's rugged interior, providing a home for Tasmanian devils and spotted-tailed quolls.

**NORTH-WEST FORESTS, TAS**

A dense forest of myrtle and eucalypts has forced individual trees to grow tall, reaching for any space in the canopy above. Shedded bark, fallen limbs, twigs and leaves litter the forest floor. The deep, aromatic oil-rich litter keeps the soil here moist, a perfect environment for fungi, and small invertebrates such as long-horned beetles and wood moths.

## LAMINGTON NP, QLD

The lush rainforest in the aptly named Green Mountains sparkles with a lustrous sheen (left and right) that signals abundant rain and fertile soil. The park's rich soils are derived from a vast extinct volcano centred on Mount Warning to the east. A long track follows Toolona Creek, passing many waterfalls, and leads to the top of Mount Bithongabel. The forest shelters creatures such the regent bowerbird (below), often heard chattering loudly or mimicking other birds.

arid lands

# arid lands

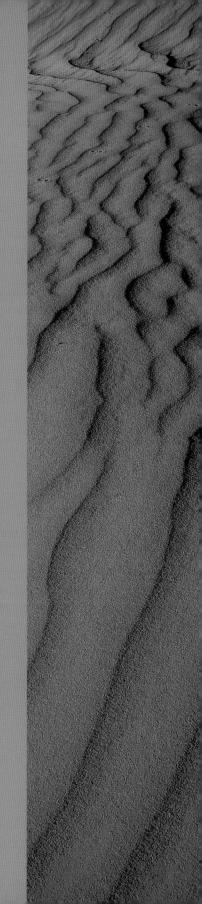

Ochres – colours drawn from palettes of red, orange and pipeclay white – are the defining hues of arid Australia. Not all the continent's out-of-the-way places are coloured in the internally lit shades of Uluru and Kata Tjuta, but equally, few scenes in climatically kinder regions glow with ochre's intrinsic warmth. The land's red regions can be pitiless places, extinguishing life with heat and aridity. But equally, they offer landscapes of unrivalled beauty, from the purity of red rock against lucent sky to the carnival riot of wildflowers.

Arid means dry, parched, withered, and by association, barren. And that, in part, describes Australia's deep inland. Yet it fails to do justice to regions where austerity frequently has a counterpoint of fresh prettiness. "...this fearful waste, this howling wilderness, this country vast and desert idle..." protested Ernest Giles in the Victoria Desert in 1875. About 85 years later, zoologist Jock Marshall wrote of central Western Australia: "The whole surface of the ground was now carpeted by flowers; hundreds of square miles of flowers. At night we camped in an enchanted land..." Enchantment is a surprisingly regular, if brief, visitor to arid lands. It may be found in a sunset that flames a range into an old-coal glow; more rarely it might be a spectacle like that of Uluru sheeted in a translucent wrapping of rainwater.

In his rebellion against a desert that would see his party go 17 days without water, Ernest Giles also saw the arid lands clearly as "...the mighty foundations of the round world laid bare." The sandstone column of Chambers Pillar is a wordless statement on the power of the wind, water and chemistry that over 350 million years has stripped away an entire landscape to leave the pillar standing 50 metres proud of the plain. The Pinnacles of coastal Western Australia, standing like tombstones recovered from the desert, instead record a mere few thousand years of water seeping through sands to create subterranean stalagmites, brought to the light by the shifting dunes.

But there are human monuments, too. Like those of the natural world, they record a slow wearing down. The arid lands are littered with the blank-eyed remains of buildings, built with stone to last. As the landscape tells us, nothing lasts, and ambitions and hopes erode more quickly than sandstone. The vast indifferent outback has blown away the buildings' histories, as it has eroded evidence of great geological events that can leave a giant boulder stranded on an inland plain. But as they fall, the buildings are forming something else – as are the boulders and ranges. As is that flock of budgerigars, breaking and swirling in a roiling cloud on the desert horizon.

*pages 140–141*

**SIMPSON DESERT, SA**

The last of the day's light ignites a dune on the southern reaches of the Simpson Desert in South Australia. This field of crimson dunes lies to the south-west of Lake Eyre North, although the prevailing winds are gradually driving the sands northwards from the Lake Eyre basin. The dunes, and the claypans that separate them, radiate ferocious heat during the day.

*page 142*

**BALGO HILLS, WA**

The red hills of Balgo look out towards the Tanami and Great Sandy deserts. Beyond the hills is a vast area of flat land, sandy dunes, spinifex and low hills. Aboriginal people have lived in the desert for thousands of years but Europeans hadn't explored it until 1856 when Augustus Gregory rode out into the desert just south of here.

*right*

**NINGALOO COAST, WA**

Driven by relentless sea breezes, this dune will eventually engulf the termite mound that stands in its way. About 5 km directly inland from Ningaloo Marine Park's dugong sanctuary, on Ningaloo Station, this is one of a series of dunes stretching from here to the coast. Very little grows here apart from the spinifex that provides the termites with food.

*left*

**CHAMBERS PILLAR, CHAMBERS PILLAR HR, NT**

Fiery molar in the desert, Chambers Pillar lights up at dawn before the sun's rays strike the scrub around it. It's easy to see why this 50 m high sandstone monolith, about 160 km due south of Alice Springs, was a useful navigation landmark for early explorers. The Pillar has always been a sacred site for Aboriginal people.

*right*

**STRZELECKI DESERT, SA**

Wind ripples and animal tracks stand out in the slanting dawn light on a Strzelecki Desert dune. Almost devoid of wildlife during the day, these dunes come alive at night with small reptiles and marsupials. This dune is near Cameron Corner, the point where NSW, SA and Queensland meet. Rising to 35 m, the dunes of the Strzelecki, which run north–south, presented a formidable obstacle to explorers pushing west.

## GIBB RIVER ROAD, WA

Like an ethereal roulette wheel, the cosmos rotates around
the south celestial pole beyond the silhouette of a giant boab
along the Gibb River Road. Far from lights and pollution, the
spectacular star shows of the outback will mesmerise you
till the first magenta glow of dawn.

*above*

**MACQUARIE MARSHES, NSW**

A spectacular light show explodes in an October night sky over the parched plains of the Macquarie Marshes. But hopes that this furious thunderstorm might ease the prevailing drought were forlorn: by morning it was gone and no rain had fallen. This area can be dry for months but bursts into life when the Macquarie River floods.

*following pages*

**KATA TJUTA, ULURU–KATA TJUTA NP, NT**

The domes of Kata Tjuta, formerly known as The Olgas, are the home of Wanambi, a mythical snake, according to the Anangu people, the area's traditional owners. Passages between the domes lead you down narrow tunnels beside towering walls where you hear the winds hum. The rocks are sacred to the Anangu and visitors are asked not to climb them.

### CONSTANCE RANGE, LAWN HILL (BOODJAMULLA) NP, QLD

Creating a palm-fringed Garden of Eden in the thirsty outback, Lawn Hill Creek emerges from the Constance Range onto the plains surrounding Boodjamulla National Park. The creek, which courses through the park's centrepiece – Lawn Hill Gorge – is spring-fed and flows year-round. As you explore the gorge by boat you're likely to spot numerous freshwater crocodiles.

**left**

## GASCOYNE, WA

In the relentless heat of summer a sunburnt claypan waits patiently for rain. Claypans like this one near the Murchison River in Western Australia's Gascoyne region come to life after rains. If you're lucky enough to visit at such a time you'll find them transformed by wildflowers.

**below**

## THORNY DEVIL

Able to change its colour to match its background, the thorny devil *(Moloch horridus)* is not nearly as menacing as it looks. This shy and harmless dragon subsists entirely on ants; its spines help defend it against predators.

**right**

## DEVILS MARBLES CR, NT

According to Aboriginal lore, the rounded boulders of this reserve are the eggs of the Rainbow Serpent, a Dreamtime being. Thousands of these boulders, which glow vividly at sunrise and sunset, lie scattered across the landscape or in heaps, often precariously balanced. Here the slender trunks of a ghost gum, one of many that dot the surrounding plains, dance in the hot morning breeze.

**FARINA, SA**

The ruins of an old hotel radiate heat in the setting sun. Like the bright hopes of those who constructed it, this hotel succumbed to the harsh realities of life in the outback. The building is one of a number in Farina, which was once a substantial township but is now deserted. The name Farina, which means flour in Latin, anticipated pastoral prosperity. But the rains didn't come.

**OXLEY STATION, MACQUARIE MARSHES, NSW**

A reminder of busier times, this classic example of outback corrugated-iron architecture glows in the late afternoon light on Oxley Station, near the southern part of the Macquarie Marshes Nature Reserve. Originally intended as a temporary home for cattlemen, the shed was abandoned many years ago. If you step inside you'll see the resident fairy martins' bottle-shaped mud nests on the ceiling.

## RAINBOW VALLEY, RAINBOW VALLEY CR, NT

Ablaze at the end of the day, the sandstone bluff of Rainbow Valley puts on a magnificent display with a palette of reds, orange, shades of gold and creamy white. The rainbow-like bands in the rock were formed by the action of water. In wet times the red iron content of the sandstone dissolved and in drier periods was drawn to the surface, creating an erosion-resistant red cap. At night you can spot the small animals of the desert, like the knob-tailed gecko below, when they emerge to hunt for food.

*left*

**PINNACLES DESERT, NAMBUNG NP, WA**

Seventeenth-century Dutch seafarers sailing along the WA coast believed these formations were the remains of an ancient city. But the structures that give this desert its name are the eroded remnants of a formerly thick bed of limestone. If you're here at night under a bright moon, shadows from the Pinnacles create a truly eerie scene.

*right*

**KARIJINI NATIONAL PARK, WA**

In late winter, a few months after a cyclone moved inland from the coast near Karratha and brought heavy rain, the Hamersley Range and its surrounds in the Pilbara region bloom with new life. Oat-eared spinifex, ground hugging mulla-mullas and the metre-high royal and giant mulla-mullas cover the plains in a carpet of pink. The display is short-lived, however, lasting only a couple of months.

*above*

**DAMPIER LAND PENINSULA, KIMBERLEY, WA**

Defying the burning heat of the Dampier Land peninsula, a stand of pandanus adorns one of the many dunes, some of them huge, in this remote part of the Kimberley. Growing in clumps, these trees look like islands in an ochre sea – a sea of sand you'll find too hot to walk on in the middle of the day.

*right*

**PALM VALLEY, FINKE GORGE NP, NT**

Relics of rainforest that flourished here 65 million years ago, central Australian cabbage palms stand tall against the walls of Palm Valley. These palms are on Palm Creek, a tributary of the Finke River. Unique to the area, they have always been sustained by the Finke, central Australia's longest river and one of the world's oldest watercourses.

# mountains & ranges

Ranges are inscribed across the Australian continent like scars on the chest of an initiated Aboriginal elder. They are vestigial remnants of geological events unimaginably large, played out over imponderable stretches of time. After long ages of weathering, Australia's mountains are now just foothills compared to the Himalaya, the Alps and the Andes. Yet the ranges' presence on a worn-down continent endows them with a grandeur that lies beyond comparisons.

Once upon a Dreamtime, two immense maned snakes moved through the landscape of what is now South Australia, intent on reaching a ceremony. The way was lit by the kingfisher, Yurlu, who had preceded them lighting coal fires. The serpents, the Akurra, found the dancing Aboriginal people, the Yura, and encircled them. The Yura fatally mistook the eyes of the Akurra for the stars; the serpents devoured the dancers, except for two who escaped, to make other stories. The bodies of the ambushing Akurra are still there today, in the cupped escarpment of Wilpena Pound; their track southward is recorded in the Flinders Ranges.

Australia's ranges enfold the scant leavings of the Aboriginal culture that thrived for tens of thousands of years before written history. Ranges gave shelter long before the era of the project home, produced in their own way the abundance of the supermarket, and embodied both the actors and plot of the theatre. What little extra Aboriginal people chose to record – given that the landscape was an ever-open encyclopaedia – was etched on the rock faces and in the caves of the hills. And when a new race swept through the continent, blind to the perfectly merged sacredness and practicality of the ranges, it was to the hills that Aboriginal people retreated, and sometimes vanished forever. Their fate is infrequently remembered in names like Darkies Leap, on the eastern escarpment of New England, but more frequently not.

For the past two centuries, Australians have loved the modest ranges and mountains of their country, if not as comprehensively as the original people then as wholeheartedly as they know how. Because there are no snowy crags thrusting through the clouds – or if they do, the illusion does not last long – there are no conquests to be made here. Heroism and climbing experience are optional extras for the ramble up to Kosciuszko's 2228 metre "peak". Australia's mountains, with a few craggy exceptions in Tasmania, are something to be enjoyed on an everyday basis. Yet the mountains continue to loom large in the Australian imagination as a source of inspiration and story; as they have always done.

*pages 174–175*

**KANANGRA WALLS, KANANGRA–BOYD NP, NSW**

The ghostly disc of a full moon rises through the lingering pink shades of twilight beyond Kanangra Gorge. The sight of Kanangra Walls at dusk, when the sandstone bluff lights up in brilliant orange, is a truly memorable experience. Two days' walk away in the distance is Mount Cloudmaker, a peak that often lives up to its name.

*page 176*

**KANANGRA WALLS, KANANGRA–BOYD NP, NSW**

Reaching out over the yawning gorge, the ramparts of Kanangra Walls trap sunset's gold beneath their overhangs. Kanangra Creek flows through the bottom of the ravine, having tumbled off Kanangra Tops at a spectacular waterfall nearby. You can enjoy this rugged wilderness as a bushwalker. Rock climbers are regular visitors here, too, drawn by some of the continent's toughest canyons.

*right*

**MORTON NP, NSW**

The conical form of Pigeon House Mountain rises from the dark-green wilderness at the southern end of one of NSW's most spectacular parks. Here the sandstone cliffs plunge hundreds of metres into the dense forest and the calls of whipbirds crack across their walls. Spectacular views like this are possible on multi-day walks through Morton and neighbouring Budawang National Park.

*left*

**FLINDERS RANGES NP, SA**

The setting sun creates a dramatic silhouette of the peaks of Wilpena Pound beyond an ancient river red gum. Wilpena is thought to be an Aboriginal word meaning cupped hand or bent fingers. The pound is a natural amphitheatre 11 km long and 5 km wide. The 300-year-old gum was made famous when it was photographed by Harold Cazneaux in 1937.

*right*

**GUY FAWKES NP, NSW**

The afternoon light paints the rugged ranges bordering the Guy Fawkes River. This spectacular wilderness area in NSW's northern highlands has dramatic escarpments that drop into steep gullies. An almost vertical track near here descends into the valley and is the start of an outstanding three-day hike. Wedge-tailed eagles often drift across the valley.

*page 182 top*

**THE CASTLE, MORTON NP, NSW**

The massive, multi-hued buttress of The Castle ends in bush that slopes down into the Yadboro Forest. The long hike to the summit, a rugged, unrelenting climb for dedicated bushwalkers, rises 750 m through forest and over boulders. You can rest under many of the rock overhangs beneath The Castle and lie listening to water dripping off the cliffs.

*page 182 bottom*

**MOUNT ARCKARINGA, SA**

Sunset bathes Mount Arckaringa in the brilliant reds, browns and yellows of the dry outback. This is the largest and most isolated of numerous startling mesas on the plains in northern South Australia, about 80 km south-west of Oodnadatta. The mountain is composed of crumbling particles that in places are reduced to sand. The summit consists of a hard silica crust.

*left*

**LIFE IN THE MOUNTAINS**

Whether they're harsh or benign, mountains and ranges
nearly always provide myriad niches for plants. Clockwise
from top left are: a snow gum bowed under its winter burden
in the Snowy Mountains, NSW; a waratah in flower on Cradle
Mountain, Tasmania; detail of a cushion plant, Mount Anne
National Park, Tasmania; the flowers of a snow gum covered
in summer snow, Mount Field National Park, Tasmania.

*right*

**THE LABYRINTH, CRADLE MOUNTAIN–LAKE
ST CLAIR NP, TAS**

Islands of green sphagnum moss appear to float on the glassy
surface of a tarn near Lake Elysia, in the Labyrinth. Even in
the middle of summer, Walled Mountain (1431 m) still shows
spots of snow. The Labyrinth is so-named because exploring
it requires you to find your way through a maze of tarns, thick
vegetation and rocky outcrops.

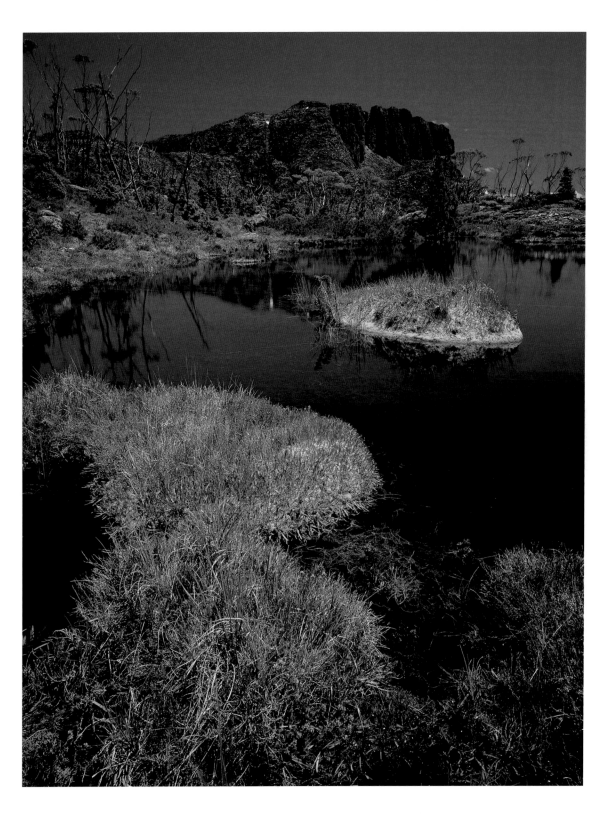

*above*

**HAMERSLEY RANGE, KARIJINI NP, WA**

Appearing to have caught a dose of rust from the iron-rich rocks in which it grows, a venerable migum tree *(Eucalyptus leucophloia)*, also called snappy gum, frames an outcrop of the Hamersley Range. The rock here began forming 2.5 billion years ago when iron oxide was deposited as sediment on the floor of an ancient sea that covered the area.

*right*

**SPY GLASS PEAK, CARNARVON NP, QLD**

Like a vast ruined building, Spy Glass Peak towers over the forested plains of the remote Salvator Rosa section of Carnarvon National Park. The banded, multicoloured sandstone wall has a hole about 10 m in diameter near the top. Sir Thomas Mitchell named the area after Salvator Rosa, the 17th-century Italian artist who created haunting images of savage scenery.

*left*

### THE THREE SISTERS, BLUE MOUNTAINS NP, NSW

The after-glow of sunset kindles the flaming sandstone hues of the Three Sisters. A favourite with visitors, the Echo Point lookout offers stunning views of the pinnacles as well as the Kedumba and Jamison valleys. It's a great place to spot birds such as the glossy black cockatoo floating over the depths.

*page 194 top*

### MOUNT KOSCIUSZKO, KOSCIUSZKO NP, NSW

In late spring, the sound of meltwater rushing down from Mount Kosciuszko fills the valley near Charlotte Pass. The runoff from Australia's highest peak (2228 m) cascades over boulders in a clear, cold torrent that eventually forms the Snowy River. After the snow melts, wombats enjoy the lush grass.

*page 194 bottom*

### POINT LOOKOUT, NEW ENGLAND NP, NSW

The rising sun bursts through haze and casts a crimson sheen over the mountain tops of this wild reserve. Standing on Point Lookout, at 1564 m the park's highest spot, is like being on top of the world. The lookout is on the edge of a plateau.

*page 195 top*

### HAMERSLEY RANGE, KARIJINI NP, WA

By darkening the shadows, late afternoon light accentuates the crumpled folds of Mount Oxer (1192 m) and the Hamersley Range. After heavy rain the runoff from the range floods the surrounding plains. Months later these open spaces erupt in the fluffy mulla-mullas that grow in abundance here.

*page 195 bottom*

### DU CANE RANGE, TAS

The knife-edged ridges of the Du Cane Range present a formidable bastion beyond the maze of the Labyrinth. The peaks of The Acropolis, on the right, and 1507 m high Mount Geryon, on the left, tower over the wide valley. To reach the Labyrinth you need to make a slow, muddy walk around Lake Ophion, on the far left.

*left*

**KEEP RIVER NP, NT**

Too hot to touch in the unrelenting afternoon sun, the banded orange domes and red walls of the ranges in this national park radiate heat across the plains. Within the range there are caves and overhangs covered in rock art created by the Miriwoong and Kadjerong people. The park, abutting the WA–NT border, provides a refuge for the endangered gouldian finch.

*right*

**PURNULULU NP, WA**

Yellow clumps of spinifex grow in bands of dots on the fire-red range in Purnululu's northern section. The massive cliffs of this west-facing range rear up suddenly from the plain. Behind them is a maze of canyons and gorges that shelter palms. The park's southern section is famous for its beehive domes (below) striped in alternating bands of orange and grey.

**WELL-WATERED RANGES**

Clouds float like spray flying from a giant green wave (left). This escarpment is in Border Ranges National Park, a World Heritage wilderness on the NSW–Queensland border. With a roar that echoes across the Jamison Valley, floodwaters surge down the normally delicate Bridal Veil Falls (above), in NSW's Blue Mountains National Park. The summit of Mount Anne (right) scrapes the sky in Tasmania's Southwest National Park. The silent alpine area is a wonderland of meadows dotted with tarns and clumps of emerald-coloured cushion plants.

# index

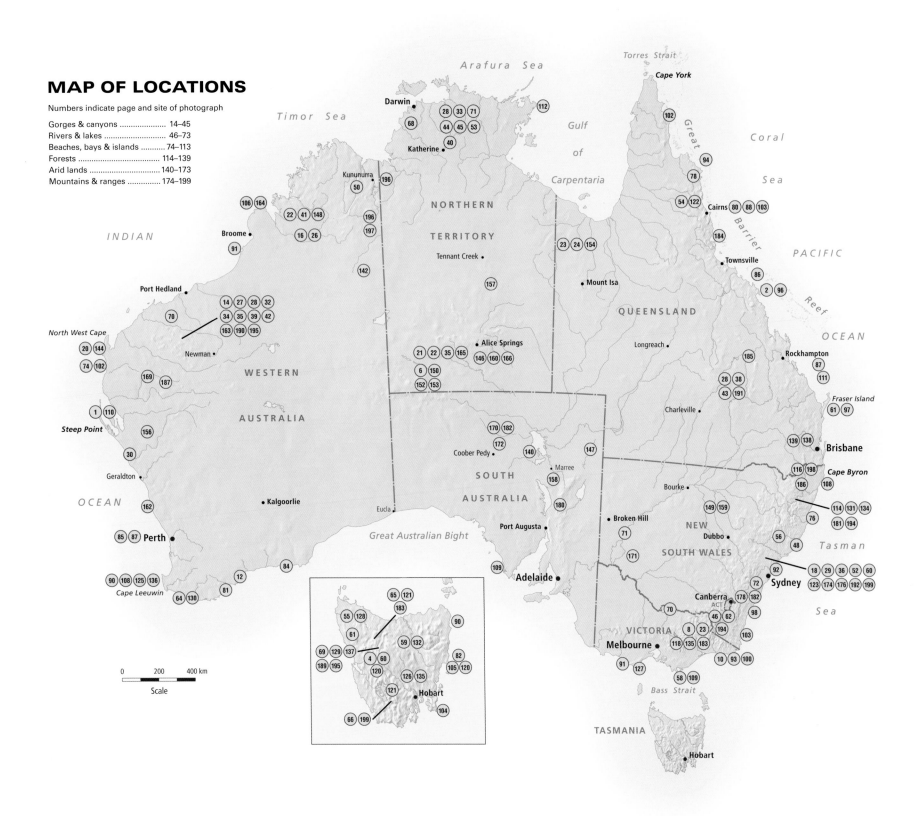

# MAP OF LOCATIONS

Numbers indicate page and site of photograph

*Torres Strait*

*Arafura Sea*

**Cape York**

*Timor Sea*

**Darwin**

28 33 71

112

68 44 45 53

40

**Katherine**

*Gulf*

*of*

*Carpentaria*

102

*Great*

94

78

Kununurra

196

50

54 122

**Cairns** 80 88 103

184

**NORTHERN**

106 164

*INDIAN*

22 41 148

196

**TERRITORY**

*Barrier*

**Townsville**

**Broome**

16 26

197

91

23 24 154

86

2 96

*Reef*

142

Tennant Creek

157

**Mount Isa**

*PACIFIC*

Port Hedland

14 27 28 32

70

34 35 39 42

163 190 195

*OCEAN*

**QUEENSLAND**

*Coral*

*Sea*

**Rockhampton**

Longreach

185

87

111

*North West Cape*

Newman

**WESTERN**

21 22 35 165

6 150

146 160 166

28 38

43 191

*Fraser Island*

20 144

74 102

169 187

**AUSTRALIA**

Charleville

61 97

1 110

139 138

**Brisbane**

*Steep Point*

156

170 182

172

**Cape Byron**

116 198

30

140

**SOUTH**

108

Geraldton

186

114 131 134

**AUSTRALIA**

76

181 194

Coober Pedy

147

85 87 **Perth**

162

Kalgoorlie

Eucla

158

**Marree**

180

Bourke

149 159

56

48

*Tasman*

*OCEAN*

**Broken Hill**

**NEW**

92 18 29 36 52 60

71

**Dubbo**

72 **Sydney** 123 174 176 192 199

*Great Australian Bight*

**Port Augusta**

109

**Adelaide**

**SOUTH WALES**

171

Canberra 178 182

ACT 98

70 46 62

84

*Sea*

12

8 23 194 103

90 108 125 136

*Cape Leeuwin*

64 130

81

**VICTORIA** 118 135 183

**Melbourne**

10 93 100

91 127

58 109

*Bass Strait*

65 121

55 128 183

61

90

59 132

69 129 137

4 60

82

189 195

120

105 120

126 135

121

**Hobart**

104

66 199

0 200 400 km

Scale

**TASMANIA**

**Hobart**

Published by Australian Geographic Pty Ltd
PO Box 321, Terrey Hills NSW 2084, Australia
Phone (02) 9473 6777; Fax (02) 9473 6701
www.australiangeographic.com.au

Managing Director: Rory Scott
Editorial Director: Dee Nolan
Managing Editor, Books: Averil Moffat

Photography: Andrew Gregory
Essays: Matthew Cawood
Captions: Andrew Gregory
Editors: Peter Meredith, Ian Connellan
Design: Susanne Geppert
Print production: Chris Roseby
Picture management: Chrissie Goldrick
Cartography: Will Pringle
Editorial assistance: Nina Paine

Text © Australian Geographic

Photography © Andrew Gregory
www.andrewgregory.com.au

Andrew thanks Marcelle for being so tireless,
his family for encouragement.

Printed in China by Toppan Printing

Copyright © Australian Geographic Pty Ltd 2005

National Library of Australia Cataloguing-in-Publication data:

Gregory, Andrew,
Colours of Australia

Includes index.
ISBN 1 86276 062 4.

1. Landscape - Australia - Pictorial works.  2. Natural
areas - Australia - Pictorial works.  3. Wilderness areas -
Australia - Pictorial works.  4. Australia - Pictorial
works.  I. Title.

919.40222

*Overleaf: Lady Musgrave Island, Great Barrier Reef, QLD*